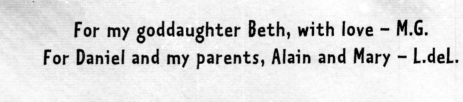

For my goddaughter Beth, with love — M.G.
For Daniel and my parents, Alain and Mary — L.deL.

First published in Great Britain and in the USA in 2007 by
Frances Lincoln Children's Books, 4 Torriano Mews,
Torriano Avenue, London NW5 2RZ
www.franceslincoln.com

Distributed in the USA by Publishers Group West

British Library Cataloguing in Publication Data available on request

The illustrations for this book are watercolour

ISBN: 978-1-84507-570-5

Printed in China

1 3 5 7 9 8 6 4 2

Stardust From Space

Monica Grady

Illustrated by Lucia deLeiris

F

FRANCES LINCOLN
CHILDREN'S BOOKS

In association with the
Natural History Museum, London

Look up at the night sky, away from the city lights, and let your eyes adjust to the darkness. Then watch as, gradually, the stars appear.

These pinpricks of light are giant balls of burning gas, millions and millions and millions of kilometres away – so far away that it can take the light thousands of years to reach us.

Suddenly there's a flash, but gone in a wink, almost before you can see it.

The flash was a shooting star, a speck of stardust, high in the atmosphere. No bigger than a grain of sand. It was moving so fast that it completely burnt away.

It was stardust that made the planets. It was stardust that built the Moon and all the stars.

So what is this dust and where did our speck of stardust come from?

The birth of a star

The Sun was made from a huge cloud of gas and dust, bigger than the whole Solar System. This cloud was just one of millions and millions that exist in space.

The cloud was squashed and collapsed, spinning round and round as more and more gas fell into the centre. It grew hotter and hotter, until the middle was so hot that it started to burn. The giant ball of burning gas was now a star, our Sun.

The new Sun was surrounded by dust, still spinning round, but now in a flat disc. The dust grains are specks of stardust. Let's follow some of these specks and see where they end up.

Building the planets

The tiny grains of stardust bang into each other, over and over again. Some of the grains stick together, making balls of dust. Some of the bigger balls become planets.

Near to the Sun, the planets are made from rock, and we call them Mercury, Venus, Earth and Mars. Further away are the gas giants, Jupiter and Saturn, then Uranus and Neptune, where it is cold enough for ice to be mixed in with the dust and gas.

Most of the stardust ended up in the Sun and the planets.

Comets: frozen wanderers in space

Do you remember the spinning disc of stardust that got so hot in the middle that it made the Sun?

Out at the furthest edge of the disc, way beyond where the planets are, it was so cold that ice formed on the specks of stardust. The dust and ice grains clumped together to make dirty snowballs. These are comets, and they orbit the Sun at the very edge of the Solar System.

Sometimes, a comet is pulled closer to the Sun, and the ice warms up. The dust that was trapped in the ice now streams out to make a tail.

The Earth, on its annual journey around the Sun, passes through the dust trails, and when that happens our skies are busy with shooting stars. The dust grains flare in a brief blaze of light as they burn up high in the Earth's atmosphere.

This is how some of our specks of stardust end – as a cosmic firework.

Asteroids: a belt of planets

Some of the specks of stardust from our disc clumped together to make small planets. These are called asteroids, and they are boulders of rock and iron that orbit the Sun between Mars and Jupiter.

Some asteroids are only a few kilometres across, whilst others are several hundred kilometres wide. Many asteroids are odd shapes. Some look like giant peanuts, tumbling end over end.

Although the asteroids are separated from each other by many thousands of kilometres of space, they do occasionally collide, and bits get knocked off. Over millions of years, their shapes have become more and more battered. Their surfaces are pitted with craters.

What happens to the chunks broken from asteroids? Most end up in the fiery graveyard of the Sun. But some plummet down to Earth, Mars, Venus and the Moon, marking their surface with craters.

Meteorites: time machines

Meteorites are chunks that have broken from asteroids
and have fallen to Earth. Meteorites fall so fast that their
outer surface gets very hot. But by the time they land,
the heat has all died away, and the meteorites are cold.

Meteorites are made from grains of stardust that clumped together when the Solar System formed. They are like time machines, taking us back to when the Solar System began. When we pick a meteorite up, we are touching one of the oldest objects within the Solar System, older than any rock on Earth.

Meteorites: uninvited guests

How many meteorites land on the Earth?
Probably a lot more than you imagine! Thousands
fall every day – but they are too small to see.
About 100 football-sized meteorites land every year –
but because most of the Earth's surface is covered
by sea, many of them are lost.

Big meteorites (about the size of a house) hit the Earth
every 100 years, and can make a pit in the ground
called a crater.

Every few million years, a really big one (maybe the size
of a small town) hits the Earth, making a crater hundreds
of kilometres across. A meteorite this size hit the Earth
65 million years ago. The explosion that it caused was
so hot and violent that many plants and animals died
in the fires that followed the explosion. Some experts
believe this explosion killed the dinosaurs.

Earth: the ground beneath our feet

Where did the Earth come from?

The Earth is a ball of squashed stardust. It got so hot in the middle (the core) that it melted, and the dust separated into iron metal. Above the core is a thick layer of very hot rock (the mantle) and on top of this is a thinner layer (the crust), which is the solid rock that we live on.

The crust is made of about 15 different plates that fit together like a jigsaw puzzle. These plates move very slowly – Europe is on a plate that is moving away from America at a speed of about 4 centimetres per year.

The stardust that made the Earth has completely changed – there are no traces of the original grains left at all.

The Moon: our nearest neighbour

The Moon is our neighbour.
Is the Moon made of stardust?
Yes it is – but it is second-hand stardust.

Not long after the Earth had formed, the Moon
was made in a huge collision between the Earth
and a giant asteroid. Enormous amounts of rock
and dust from the crash were thrown out into space,
and spun into a ring that circled round the Earth.
Eventually, the ring collapsed into a ball,
and made the Moon, which still circles round
the Earth.

At first, the Moon was rocked by volcanic
eruptions, leaving vast flows of lava over its
surface. Now the surface of the Moon is still
and dead, covered in dust.

Astronauts have visited the Moon, stirring up
powdery layers of dust as they explored.
They brought moondust back to Earth
that once was stardust.

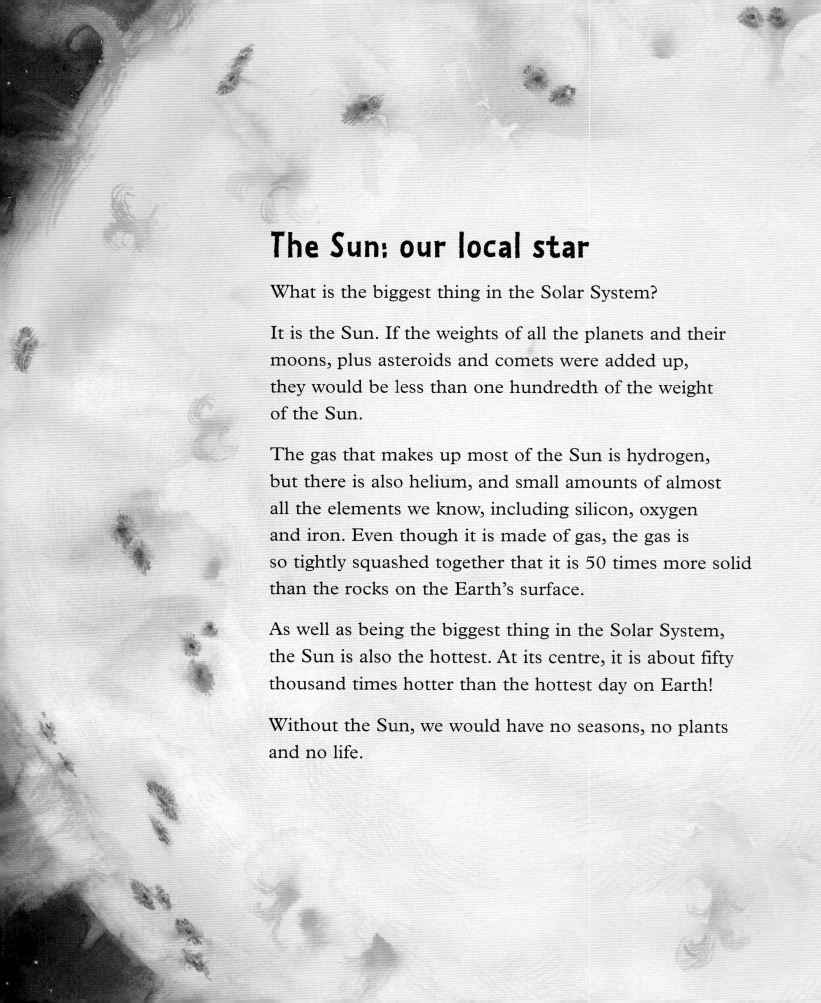

The Sun: our local star

What is the biggest thing in the Solar System?

It is the Sun. If the weights of all the planets and their
moons, plus asteroids and comets were added up,
they would be less than one hundredth of the weight
of the Sun.

The gas that makes up most of the Sun is hydrogen,
but there is also helium, and small amounts of almost
all the elements we know, including silicon, oxygen
and iron. Even though it is made of gas, the gas is
so tightly squashed together that it is 50 times more solid
than the rocks on the Earth's surface.

As well as being the biggest thing in the Solar System,
the Sun is also the hottest. At its centre, it is about fifty
thousand times hotter than the hottest day on Earth!

Without the Sun, we would have no seasons, no plants
and no life.

The death of a star

Stars burn gas, and eventually the fuel runs out.
The Sun has been burning for over 4560 million years,
and is about halfway through its lifetime. The Sun is
only a small star, so it will gradually become cooler,
expanding first into a red giant star, before collapsing
to a white dwarf.

Stars much bigger than the Sun suddenly explode
as a bright fireball, completely destroying the star.
This is called a supernova. But that is not the end.
As the star explodes, dust and gas are thrown out
in all directions. The dust is swept throughout
space, ready to act as a building block
for new stars and planets.

Without supernova explosions,
new stars and new
planets would
never form.

And so the cycle starts again –
dust into stars, then stars into dust.
These specks of stardust, smaller than a pinhead,
fall through space. They have come from a dead
star and will soon become part of a new one.

Glossary

Asteroid: a small object orbiting the Sun mostly between Mars and Jupiter. There are many thousands of asteroids. The biggest is called Ceres, and is almost 1000 kilometres (620 miles) across.

Astronaut: a person who travels in space.

Comet: a primitive rock of ice and dust that orbits the Sun.

Core: the central part of a planet. This may be molten or solid.

Cosmic dust: small particles less than 1mm in size produced from asteroids and comets, and are also called micrometeorites or interplanetary dust.

Crust: the outermost solid layer of a planet.

Element: a substance that is made from atoms of only one type.

Lava: molten rock that comes from a volcano.

Mantle: the layer above the core, but below the crust of a planet.

Meteorite: a rocky or metal object that survives its fall to Earth from space.

Moon: with a capital 'M' it is the Earth's moon and with a small 'm' is the moon of any other planet.

Planet: a large object orbiting the Sun. There are eight planets in the Solar System. In order of distance from the Sun, they are Mercury, Venus, Earth, Mars, Jupiter, Saturn, Uranus and Neptune. Pluto is sometimes classed as a planet, but it is more correct to class it as a Kuiper Belt object. These are objects of rock and ice that orbit the Sun beyond Neptune.

Plate: the rigid blocks of Earth's crust that move at very slow speeds over the Earth's surface. When they move away from each other they produce new crust when hot rock from the mantle cools and fills the gap left behind. Sometimes one plate will push part of another down into the mantle where it melts. Plates can also collide with each other, causing the crust to be uplifted to form mountains.

Shooting Star: a speck of dust that completely burns up as it travels through the atmosphere. It is also called a meteoroid.

Solar System: the Sun, the planets, their moons, and all other objects that orbit the Sun.

Star: intensely hot objects that produce energy by burning gas (mainly hydrogen).

Supernova: a sudden, rapid explosion of a star, throwing matter and energy into space.

Volcano: an opening in a planet or moon's crust through which molten rock and gas can escape.